Published by Paperview Europe Ltd.

Printed and bound by
Leo Paper Products Ltd.

DINOSAURS

How Your Encyclopedia Works

 Mickey, Minnie, Donald, Daisy, Goofy and Pluto are ready to take you on an adventure ride through the world of learning. Discover the secrets of science, nature, our world, the past and much more. Climb aboard and enjoy the ride.

Look here for a general summary of the theme

Labels tell you what's happening in the pictures

The pictures by themselves can tell you a lot, even before you read a word

Mickey's ears *lead you to one of the main topics*

Watch out for special pages where Mickey takes a close look at some key ideas

The Solar Sys[tem]

The Solar System is the [name] given to our Sun and its fam[ily of] planets. It also includes the [Sun's] moons, millions of pieces of [rock] called asteroids and meteor[s] and frozen lumps of dust an[d ice] called comets. Everything el[se you] can see in the sky is outside [the] Solar System and is far, far away. Every single star is itself a sun, and each may have its own family of planets and moons.

Saturn is surrounded

REPTILES AND AMPHIBIANS

Color and Camouflage

Frogs and toads come in nearly every imaginable color, even gold or black. They have a wide range of patterns, from spots and stripes to zigzags.

Color and pattern help frogs and toads survive. Bright colors warn that they may be poisonous. Drab colors camouflage them, or hide them against their background. Many tree frogs are exactly the same green as leaves, while others look like bark. The Asian horned toad has the best camouflage of all. Folds of patchy, brown skin and a flat body make it look like a dead leaf when it lies still on the forest floor.

Folds of brown skin give perfect camouflage

Flat body is hard to see among dead leaves

Asian horned toad

False-eyed frog

Markings look like eyes

For extra protection, bad-smelling liquid oozes out around false eyes

FALSE-EYED FROG
The South American false-eyed frog has large markings on its flanks that look like eyes. These fool some predators into thinking that they are looking at a much larger animal, such as a cat or bird.

COLOR AND CAMOUFLAGE

Dog sniffing curiously at the toad

Oriental fire-bellied toad defending itself against a dog

Skin oozes a stinging fluid

Bright colored belly

Green and black back

FIRE-BELLIED TOAD
When cornered by a predator, the Oriental fire-bellied toad of eastern Asia arches its back and rears up on its legs to show its fiery underside. Wise attackers back off, because the toad's skin oozes a stinging, bad-tasting fluid.

Toad rears up on its back legs

Strawberry arrow frog

POISON-DART FROGS
Deadly poison oozes from the skin of Central and South American poison-dart frogs. People in the rain forest rub the tips of their arrows and blowpipe darts on the skin of these frogs to collect the poison to use for hunting.

Blue poison-dart frog

FIND OUT MORE
MAMMALS: Camouflage
PLANET EARTH: Forests

16

17

Mickey's page *numbers help you look things up. Don't forget there's a glossary and index at the back of each book*

Goofy and his *friends know how to give you a chuckle on every topic*

Mickey points you to more information in other books in your *Encyclopedia*

FIND OUT MORE
THE KINGDOM OF MAMMALS: Camouflage
PLANET EARTH: Forests

AMAZING FACTS
★ The Sun is enormous compared to the planets. It is nearly 1,000 times more massive than the giant planet Jupiter.

Your favourite characters present some facts to astound you and your friends

Numbers lead *you step-by-step through how things happen*

Colourful boxes *zoom in on information*

Mickey's helpers test some ideas themselves

THE SOLAR SYSTEM

HOW OUR SOLAR SYSTEM WAS FORMED

AMAZING FACTS
★ The Sun is enormous compared to the planets. It is nearly 1,000 times more massive than the giant planet Jupiter.

1 The Solar System formed 4.6 billion years ago. It started at the centre of an enormous swirling cloud of gas and dust.

2 The Sun burst into flames and became a star. Its light and warmth spread throughout the new Solar System.

3 Gas and dust left over from making the Sun clumped together in places. These clumps grew bigger and formed the planets.

4 The planets closest to the Sun are small and made from rock and metal. The larger outer planets are made from gas and liquid.

Pluto was the farthest planet from the Sun until 2006, when it was reclassified as a minor planet

Each planet has its own path, or orbit

Planet orbits

ORBITING THE SUN
No matter how still you try to be, you are always moving. This is because the Earth – and all the other planets – are moving. They are flying through Space around the Sun in looping paths called orbits.

Neptune is a cold, blue planet

Uranus is tipped over on its side

THE "PULL" OF GRAVITY
If you throw a ball into the air, it comes down again. The invisible force that pulls it down to Earth is called gravity. The Earth's gravity holds us down on the ground. The Sun's gravity is strong enough to hold all its planets in their orbits.

Gravity pulls a ball to Earth

ars is red d dusty

The Solar System

FIND OUT MORE
PLANET EARTH: Night and day
THE MARVELS OF SCIENCE: Gravity

Contents

INTRODUCING
Dinosaurs

Long before humans appeared, reptiles
called dinosaurs roamed and ruled the
Earth. Theirs was a very different world
from ours, and many different types of
dinosaurs learned to live among the
thick forests and on the vast plains.

Small and speedy hunters chased after prey.
Giant plant-eaters gobbled the leaves and flowers.
Some of these reptiles took to the water, and
some learned to fly. Then, suddenly and
mysteriously, they all disappeared.

The Dinosaur Era

Dinosaur

Dinosaurs were the most successful animals that ever lived. They were the rulers of life on Earth for an amazing 165 million years. Humans have been around for only about 100,000 years, so far. The first dinosaurs appeared 230 million years ago. The last of these creatures died out about 65 million years ago.

Straight legs

Lizard

Splayed legs

DINOSAURS WERE REPTILES

Dinosaurs were reptiles that lived on land. Most reptiles (such as lizards) have leathery or scaly skin and lay eggs with hard shells. Their legs sprawl out sideways. Dinosaurs held their legs straight below their bodies and could carry more weight, so they became larger and faster.

AMACING FACTS

★ When huge fossil dinosaur bones were first found in China hundreds of years ago, people thought they must be the bones of giant dragons.

DINOSAURS DIED OUT

Dinosaurs mysteriously all died out at the end of the Mesozoic era. This gave mammals their chance to take over. Mammals often have fur, and they usually give birth to live babies (not eggs) that feed on their mothers' milk. Humans are mammals.

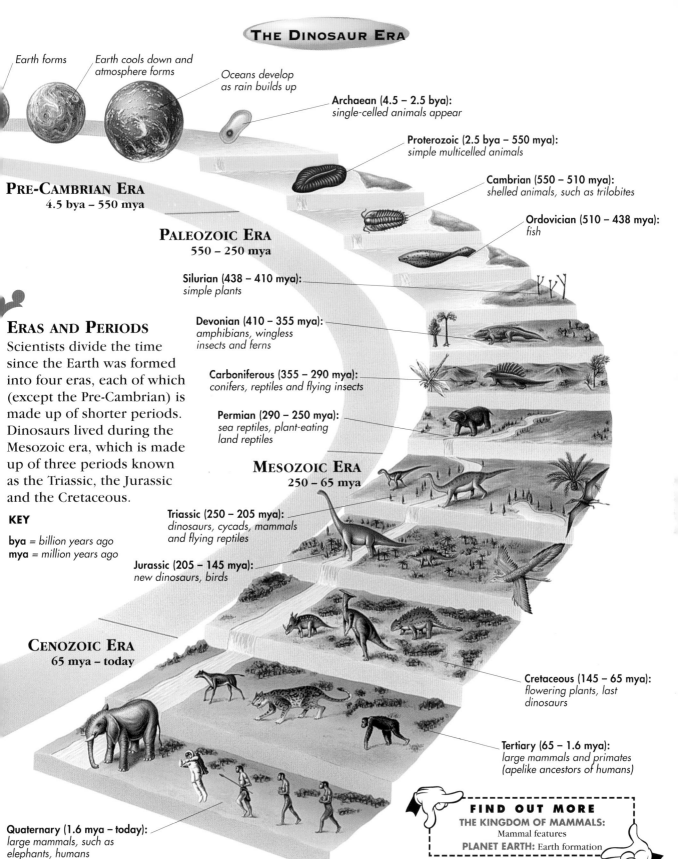

Earth forms

Earth cools down and atmosphere forms

Oceans develop as rain builds up

Archaean (4.5 – 2.5 bya): single-celled animals appear

Proterozoic (2.5 bya – 550 mya): simple multicelled animals

Cambrian (550 – 510 mya): shelled animals, such as trilobites

Ordovician (510 – 438 mya): fish

PRE-CAMBRIAN ERA
4.5 bya – 550 mya

PALEOZOIC ERA
550 – 250 mya

Silurian (438 – 410 mya): simple plants

Devonian (410 – 355 mya): amphibians, wingless insects and ferns

Carboniferous (355 – 290 mya): conifers, reptiles and flying insects

Permian (290 – 250 mya): sea reptiles, plant-eating land reptiles

MESOZOIC ERA
250 – 65 mya

ERAS AND PERIODS

Scientists divide the time since the Earth was formed into four eras, each of which (except the Pre-Cambrian) is made up of shorter periods. Dinosaurs lived during the Mesozoic era, which is made up of three periods known as the Triassic, the Jurassic and the Cretaceous.

KEY

bya = billion years ago
mya = million years ago

Triassic (250 – 205 mya): dinosaurs, cycads, mammals and flying reptiles

Jurassic (205 – 145 mya): new dinosaurs, birds

CENOZOIC ERA
65 mya – today

Cretaceous (145 – 65 mya): flowering plants, last dinosaurs

Tertiary (65 – 1.6 mya): large mammals and primates (apelike ancestors of humans)

Quaternary (1.6 mya – today): large mammals, such as elephants, humans

FIND OUT MORE
THE KINGDOM OF MAMMALS: Mammal features
PLANET EARTH: Earth formation

The First Dinosaurs

The earliest of the dinosaurs appeared in the second half of the Triassic period, which lasted from 250 million to 205 million years ago. At this time, the world looked very different from the way it is today because the land was all in one big piece, called Pangaea. There were no seas to block the way, so the Triassic dinosaurs were able to travel easily across the land. They were soon living all over the world.

The Triassic world

Land | Shallow sea | Deep sea

TRIASSIC ANIMALS

Some of the first dinosaurs were large plant-eaters. These were the first creatures large enough to feed on leaves high up in the branches of tall plants. They shared the Triassic world with other kinds of land reptiles and with the first flying reptiles.

Plateosaurus, *a large plant-eating dinosaur*

Tree fern

Thrinaxodon, *a mammal-like reptile*

TRIASSIC WEATHER REPORT

It was mild and warm everywhere during the Triassic. Some areas were very far from the sea and from rain-carrying winds. This made them dry, with little life. There were no ice caps at either of the Earth's poles.

Eudimorphodon,
a small flying reptile

Massospondylus,
a large plant-eating dinosaur

AMAZING FACTS

★ The first mammals appeared toward the end of the Triassic, but they were only small creatures and looked a bit like shrews.

Conifers

Cycad

PLANTS OF THE TIME

Tree ferns were common and so were cycads – plants that looked like palm trees. Conifers were the tallest of the trees. There were no flowering plants or grasses anywhere in the Triassic.

Ornithosuchus,
a reptile

FIND OUT MORE
PLANET EARTH: Pangaea
PLANTS ARE AMAZING: Conifers

Reign of the Dinosaurs

Dinosaurs ruled the world in the Jurassic (205 million to 145 million years ago). The large land mass, Pangaea, started breaking into two continents. Many remarkable new dinosaurs came into existence. Plants grew big in the warm, wet climate, so there was plenty of food for the animals that fed on them. A plant-eater that reached more than 30 m (100 ft) long could probably eat its way through as much as a ton of leaves a day.

The Jurassic world

Land — Shallow sea — Deep sea

Archaeopteryx, the first known bird, was a poor flyer

Cycad

JURASSIC ANIMALS

Plant-eating, plated dinosaurs such as *Stegosaurus* and sharp-toothed hunters like *Yangchuanosaurus*, appeared during the Jurassic. Flying reptiles shared the sky with the first bird, *Archaeopteryx*, which had feathers, but was probably a poor flyer. To take off, it had to climb a tree and then leap into the air.

AMAZING FACTS

★ Unlike birds today, *Archaeopteryx* did not have a beak. Instead, it had jaws lined with small, sharp teeth for eating insects.

JURASSIC PLANTS

Ferns were the most common low-growing plants of the Jurassic. They covered huge areas of the land. Cycads and conifers similar to today's giant sequoia trees filled the forests.

Conifers

Barapasaurus,
a giant plant-eating dinosaur

Stegosaurus,
a plant-eating plated dinosaur

Pterodactylus,
a flying reptile

Fern

WARM AND WET

Earth's climate was still warm and mild in the Jurassic, but there was also plenty of rain. Shallow seas spread across parts of the land, and some of the inland deserts of the Triassic disappeared.

FIND OUT MORE
PLANET EARTH: Climates
PLANTS ARE AMAZING: Ferns

Yangchuanosaurus,
a big, meat-eating dinosaur

A Changing World

Great changes took place in the Cretaceous (145 – 65 million years ago). The land was splitting up, forming new continents. Flowering plants appeared and spread fast. Soon there were new kinds of plant-eating dinosaurs to eat them. This meant plenty of food for the meat-eaters, which grew in number too.

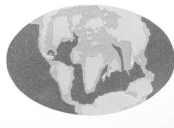

The Cretaceous world

Land — Shallow sea — Deep sea

Ichthyosaurus, *a sea reptile*

ANIMALS OF THE CRETACEOUS
Huge hunting dinosaurs walked the land. Soaring above them were birds and big, flying reptiles. Reptiles called ichthyosaurs swam in the sea.

Corythosaurus, *a plant-eating duckbill dinosaur*

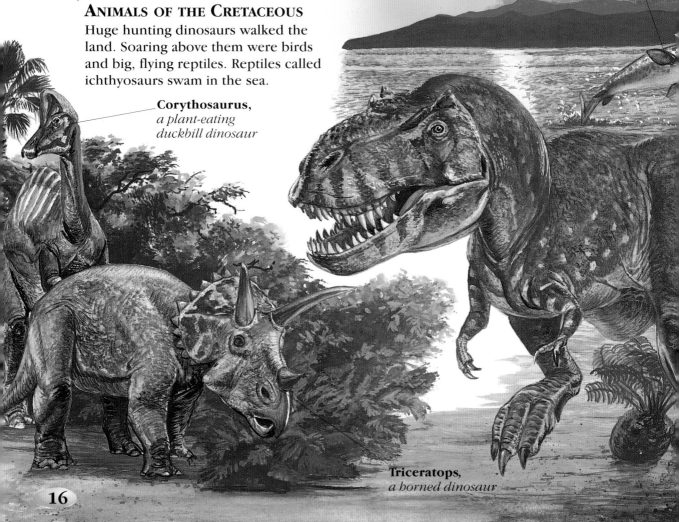

Triceratops, *a horned dinosaur*

16

Pteranodon,
a flying reptile

A CHANGING CLIMATE

Early in the Cretaceous, the weather was always warm, although there were wet and dry seasons each year. Later in the period, when the world became cooler, some areas began to have summers and winters.

AMAZING FACTS

★ The *Pteranodon's* outstretched wings measured about 7 m (23 ft) from tip to tip. That is twice as long as the average family car.

Ichthyornis,
a bird

FLOWERING PLANTS

Flowering plants, such as magnolia, probably first grew near the Equator 120 million years ago. Bees and other new flying insects spread pollen, and soon flowers were common everywhere. Ferns and cycads now became much less common.

Tarbosaurus,
a large hunting dinosaur

Flowering plants

FIND OUT MORE
INSECTS AND SPIDERS: Bees
PLANTS ARE AMAZING: Flowering plants

Finding Out About Dinosaurs

No one has ever seen a living dinosaur because dinosaurs died out millions of years before humans appeared on Earth. But we know they existed from the many fossils that have been found all over the world.

Fossils are the remains of long-dead plants and animals preserved in rock. Bones and teeth are the most common dinosaur fossils, but many fossilized droppings, eggs, footprints and skin markings have also been found. Most fossils are discovered by experts called paleontologists – scientists who study prehistoric life. They piece together the bones and other evidence to learn as much as they can about dinosaurs.

Fossil dinosaur droppings

Fossil imprint of dinosaur skin

DIGGING UP THE BONES

Fossil dinosaur bones must be taken from the surrounding rock with great care, using tools ranging from chisels to soft brushes. Sections of rock containing large bones are wrapped in sacking and plaster of Paris to protect them during transport.

Every bone is photographed before it is removed

Large bones wrapped in plaster need careful handling

Workers wrap a bone in sacking and plaster

FROM DINOSAUR TO FOSSIL

1 A dinosaur dies, then its flesh rots away, leaving only the bones.

2 The bones are slowly buried under layers of mud and sand.

3 Mud, sand and bones turn to rock over millions of years.

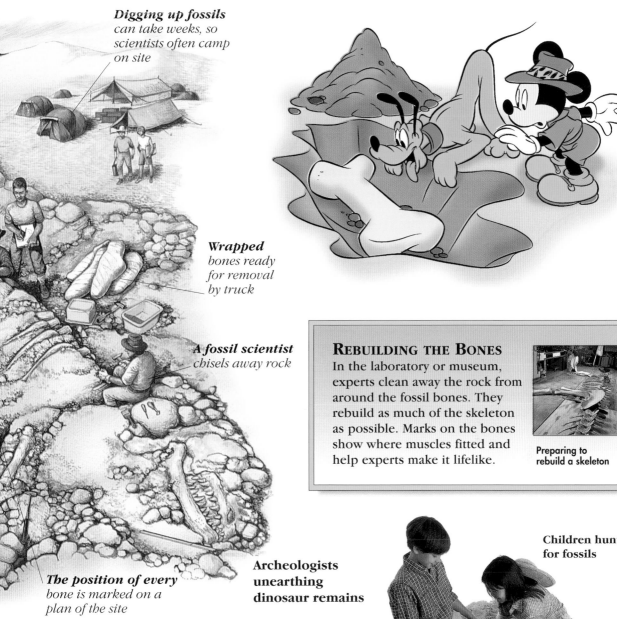

Digging up fossils *can take weeks, so scientists often camp on site*

Wrapped *bones ready for removal by truck*

A fossil scientist *chisels away rock*

The position of every *bone is marked on a plan of the site*

REBUILDING THE BONES

In the laboratory or museum, experts clean away the rock from around the fossil bones. They rebuild as much of the skeleton as possible. Marks on the bones show where muscles fitted and help experts make it lifelike.

Preparing to rebuild a skeleton

Archeologists unearthing dinosaur remains

Children hunting for fossils

Tools

FIND YOUR OWN FOSSILS

Anyone can be a fossil-hunter, even if not everyone can dig up dinosaurs. Try looking on a beach, or in other places where there are rocks such as sandstone. All you need are simple tools like a hammer and chisel. Ask an adult to help you split rocks, and you might find wonderful fossils inside.

4 **The rock layers** are worn away by wind and rain, exposing the harder, fossilized bones.

FIND OUT MORE
PLANET EARTH: Fossils
FROM STONE AGE TO SPACE AGE:
Archeological digs

Giant Plant-eaters

👉The giant plant-eating sauropods were the biggest and heaviest dinosaurs of all. They included the largest land animals that have ever lived. Most had small heads, long necks and long tails. Their huge bodies were supported on thick legs the size of tree trunks. Sauropods probably roamed in herds, feeding on huge numbers of plants.

Brachiosaurus:
length 30 m (100 ft)

GIANT *BRACHIOSAURUS*
Brachiosaurus was a gigantic plant-eater that may have weighed more than 80 tons. This is heavier than 12 African elephants. Its front legs were longer than its back legs, so its body sloped toward the tail, like that of a giraffe.

Short back legs

SAUROPOD TYPES
There were at least six kinds of sauropod. The cetiosaurs appeared first, in the Jurassic. Brachiosaurs were the heavyweights. Diplodocids were big, but lighter in weight. Camarasaurs were much smaller. Titanosaurs appeared last, living to the end of the Cretaceous.

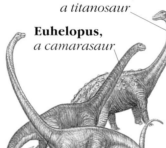

Saltasaurus, *a titanosaur*

Euhelopus, *a camarasaur*

Mamenchisaurus, *a diplodocid*

LIGHT-BONED GIANTS
Each bone, or vertebra, in a giant plant-eater's spine has scooped-out sides. This design makes the spine bones light, yet strong. The brachiosaurs show this clearly.

Brachiosaur vertebra

Brachiosaur with young

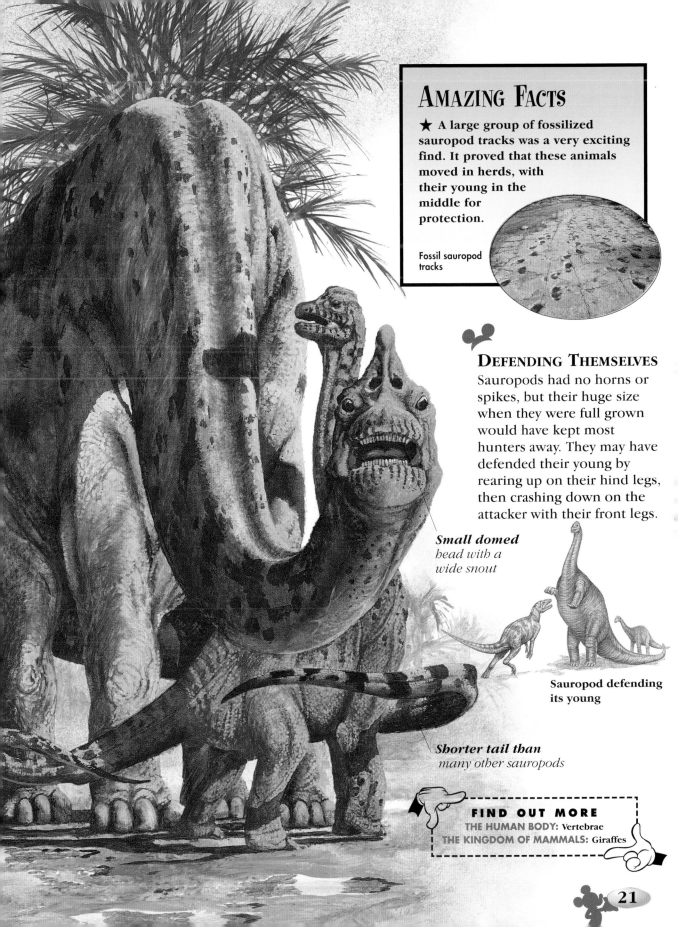

DEFENDING THEMSELVES

Sauropods had no horns or spikes, but their huge size when they were full grown would have kept most hunters away. They may have defended their young by rearing up on their hind legs, then crashing down on the attacker with their front legs.

Small domed *head with a wide snout*

Sauropod defending its young

Shorter tail than *many other sauropods*

FIND OUT MORE
THE HUMAN BODY: Vertebrae
THE KINGDOM OF MAMMALS: Giraffes

21

Small Hunters

 Some hunting dinosaurs, such as the ceratosaurs, coelurosaurs and oviraptors, were surprisingly small and light. They ran on their back legs, leaving their strong arms and claws free for seizing lizards and small mammals. Experts think birds may have developed from small, fast dinosaurs like these.

Coelophysis:
length 3 m (10 ft)

AMAZING FACTS

★ *Saltopus*, one of the ceratosaurs, was just 60 cm (24 in) long and would have weighed only about 2 kg (4 lb).

DINOSAUR CANNIBAL

Among the ribs of this *Coelophysis* fossil are the tiny bones of a baby *Coelophysis*. This may mean the dinosaur was a cannibal that ate the young of other *Coelophysis*.

Tail held out straight for balance when running

MINI DINOSAUR

One of the smallest of all known dinosaurs was *Compsognathus*. Just 70 cm (28 in) long, including its tail, it was only as tall as a hen. This coelurosaur probably hunted insects and lizards, which it would have caught in its long, slender jaws.

NOT AN EGG THIEF

The first *Oviraptor* fossil was found with eggs. Experts at the time thought *Oviraptor* was stealing the eggs from another dinosaur, *Protoceratops*. Now they think it was guarding its own eggs when it died.

Child studying model of *Compsognathus*

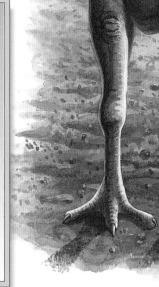

PACK HUNTERS

Coelophysis lived on dry plains in North America. It probably moved along swiftly, in packs, hunting small animals. Hunting in groups would have given *Coelophysis* some protection against bigger hunters. Although it was larger than many ceratosaurs, it was still slender and lightly built.

Slender neck
is flexible

Long jaws lined
*with sharp,
serrated teeth*

**Coelophysis
hunting together**

Long fingers
for grasping prey

Long, slender legs
for speed and agility

FIND OUT MORE
THE KINGDOM OF MAMMALS:
First mammals
REPTILES AND AMPHIBIANS: Lizards

23

Fast-running Hunters

👉 Among the fastest dinosaurs were the dromaeosaurs and ornithomimids, which lived in the Cretaceous. The fierce dromaeosaurs had powerful jaws and large curving claws that may have helped them to attack much larger dinosaurs. Ornithomimids looked like modern ostriches. They probably ran very fast, snapping up small animals in toothless jaws that looked like beaks.

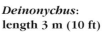

Deinonychus:
length 3 m (10 ft)

FIERCE HUNTERS

The agile dromaeosaur *Deinonychus* probably hunted in ferocious packs and killed much larger dinosaurs, like *Iguanodon*. Hanging onto their victim by their front claws, they could have slashed through its thick skin with the deadly curved claw on each back foot.

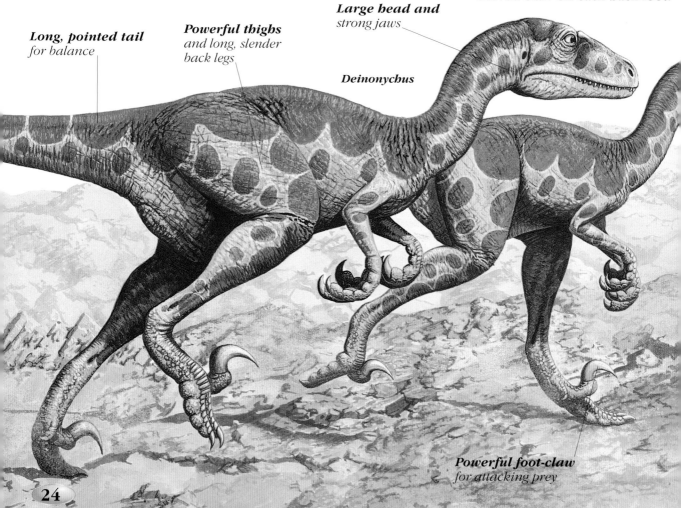

Long, pointed tail
for balance

Powerful thighs
and long, slender back legs

Large head and
strong jaws

Deinonychus

Powerful foot-claw
for attacking prey

FAST RUNNERS

Long-legged *Ornithomimus* and other ornithomimids looked much like today's fast-moving ostriches. Like them, they would have run long distances looking for food. Speed would also have helped them escape other hunters.

Ostriches can run at 65 km/h (40 mph)

Ornithomimus

AMAZING FACTS

★ A dromaeosaur's special weapons – the curved claws on its feet – were about 15 cm (6 in) long.

JAGGED-TOOTHED HUNTER

The dromaeosaur *Velociraptor* had strong jaws lined with large, backward-curving teeth. These teeth had jagged edges for cutting into flesh. *Velociraptor* fossils have been found in China and Mongolia.

Velociraptor jaw with teeth

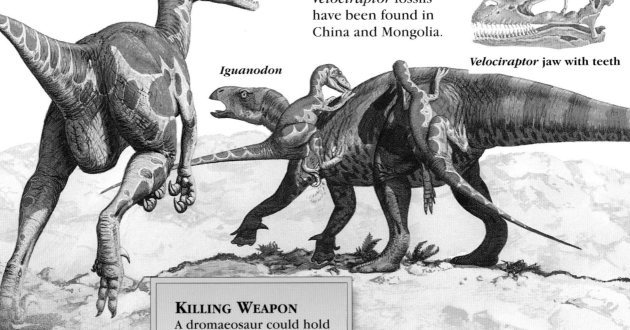

Iguanodon

Pack of *Deinonychus* attacking a single *Iguanodon*

KILLING WEAPON

A dromaeosaur could hold its foot-claws clear of the ground when running, then swing them down when slashing at prey.

Claw held clear of ground

Claw in slashing position

FIND OUT MORE
THE HUMAN BODY: Teeth
BIRDS: Ostrich

Dinosaur Skeletons

Fossil bones and teeth are all that remain of dinosaurs today – but experts can rebuild the skeletons using their knowledge of living animals.

The shape and size of a dinosaur's teeth and bones show whether it ate plants or meat, and whether it walked on four legs or ran on two. When some of the bones are missing, experts can often reconstruct them by studying the complete skeletons of other, similar dinosaurs. But some dinosaurs are a mystery. Fossil arm bones 2.5 m (8 ft) long, with huge claws, were found in Mongolia over 30 years ago. No one knows what this *Deinocheirus* looked like because nothing else like it has been found anywhere in the world.

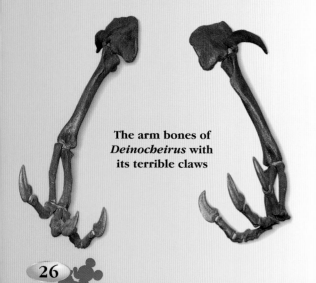

The arm bones of *Deinocheirus* with its terrible claws

Children are small compared to the size of an *Iguanodon* skeleton

IGUANODON SKELETON

The skeleton of *Iguanodon* was strong and sturdy enough to support this large plant-eater, which weighed as much as an African elephant. So many *Iguanodon* skeletons have been found that experts have a very good idea of what the animal must have looked like when it was alive.

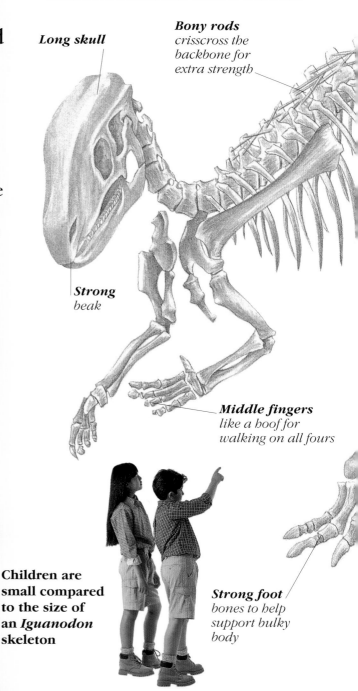

Long skull

Bony rods crisscross the backbone for extra strength

Strong beak

Middle fingers like a hoof for walking on all fours

Strong foot bones to help support bulky body

Plant-eater

Meat-eater

DIFFERENT DIETS

Experts know what dinosaurs ate by looking at their skulls. Meat-eaters had strong jaws full of big, sharp teeth – often with jagged, slicing edges. Most plant-eaters had toothless beaks for chopping off plants and broad, flat back teeth for grinding them up.

Long tail held out
straight for balance when Iguanodon *was on two legs*

FILLING IN THE GAPS

Whole fossils are rare. When a new dinosaur, *Baryonyx*, was found in 1986, many missing bones had to be filled in.

Fossil bones (brown)

Missing bones (blue)

Backbone

Bones below
tail to protect blood vessels running under the backbone

Hip bone

LEG AND FEET BONES

Giant plant-eaters walked on all four legs. Because of their great weight, these dinosaurs had to have very solid legs and short, thick ankle bones. The smaller and lighter meat-eaters had slender legs with long, slim ankle bones so they could run fast to catch their food.

Heavy leg bones
needed to support the animal's weight

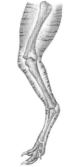

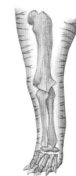

Light, meat-eating dinosaur

Giant plant-eater

FIND OUT MORE
THE HUMAN BODY: Skeleton
THE KINGDOM OF MAMMALS:
African elephant

Giant Hunters

The biggest hunting dinosaurs were the carnosaurs – the largest meat-eating animals known to have lived on land. Carnosaurs such as *Tyrannosaurus* were heavy animals with big, powerful heads, strong jaws and lots of teeth as sharp as daggers. They walked on incredibly powerful back legs and were always ready to run to attack passing dinosaurs. Strangely, their front legs were tiny – too short even to reach their mouths.

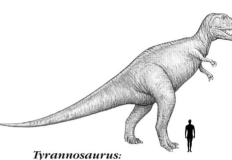

Tyrannosaurus:
length 12 m (40 ft)

ON THE ATTACK

Mighty *Tyrannosaurus* lived in North America during the Cretaceous. Too heavy to run far, it may have hidden in wait for a large plant-eater. It would then have dashed forward and killed its victim with a bite to the neck.

NEW-FOUND GIANTS

Two huge new carnosaurs were discovered in 1995 – *Carcharodontosaurus* and *Gigantosaurus*. Their massive skulls and huge, pointed teeth were even bigger than those of *Tyrannosaurus*.

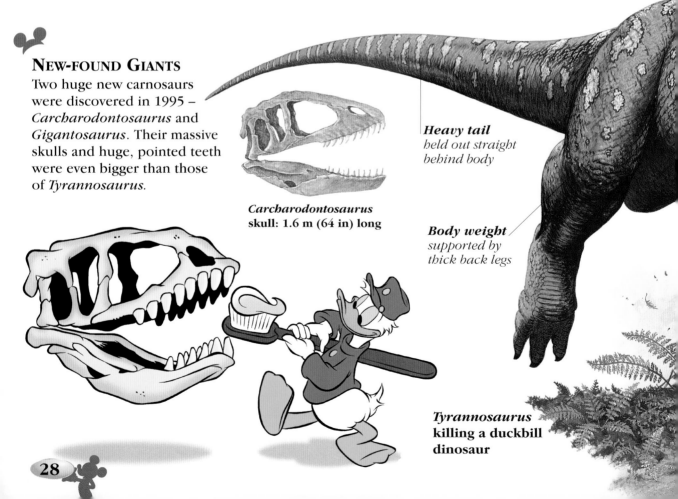

Heavy tail
held out straight behind body

Body weight
supported by thick back legs

Carcharodontosaurus
skull: 1.6 m (64 in) long

***Tyrannosaurus*
killing a duckbill
dinosaur**

Tiny front legs with two small claws

CARNOTAURUS

Discovered in Argentina in 1985, *Carnotaurus* was about 7.5 m (25 ft) long. This dinosaur was similar to *Tyrannosaurus*, but it had a deeper head and there were small horns above its eyes.

Carnotaurus

Rows of scales on its back and sides

STAYING SHARP

Carnosaurs needed to have very sharp teeth all the time. This jaw bone from *Megalosaurus* shows how sharp new teeth would grow through to replace any that were old or worn.

New tooth   Old tooth

Strong, broad chest

Flexible neck

Jaw filled with 60 jagged teeth

AMAZING FACTS

★ The biggest carnosaurs, such as *Tyrannosaurus* and *Carcharodontosaurus*, may have weighed as much as 8 tons – more than an African elephant.

Duckbill dinosaur was easy prey

FIND OUT MORE
THE KINGDOM OF MAMMALS: Skulls
THE HUMAN BODY: Teeth

Peaceful Plant-eaters

Plant-eaters called iguanodonts lived in nearly all parts of the world during the Jurassic and the Cretaceous. These peaceful creatures probably moved in herds, eating ferns and other plants. They were solid animals with thick legs, heavy tails and long heads. They had strong beaks, as well as a set of teeth farther back in their jaws for grinding down tough food.

Iguanodon:
length 9 m (30 ft)

ON FOUR LEGS OR TWO

Iguanodon probably walked slowly on four legs most of the time. It may also have run on its strong back legs to escape from danger. When it stood on two legs to reach food, its long tail would have helped the animal balance.

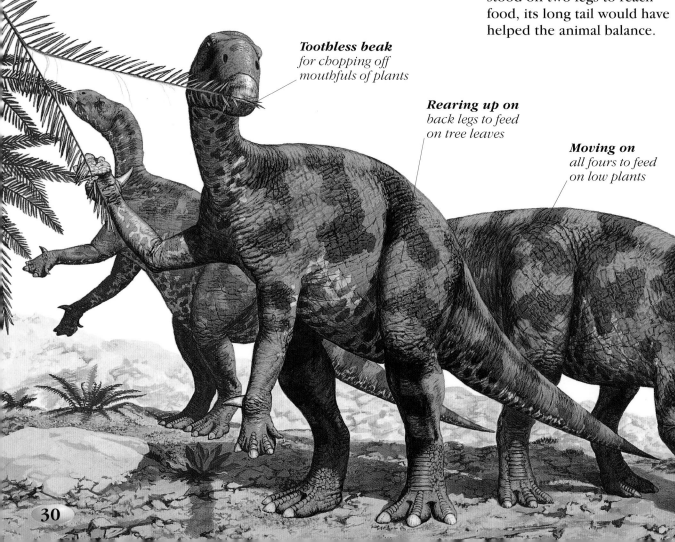

Toothless beak
for chopping off mouthfuls of plants

Rearing up on
back legs to feed on tree leaves

Moving on
all fours to feed on low plants

Bony bump

Muttaburrasaurus

AMAZING FACTS

★ *Iguanodon* was only the second dinosaur to be given a name (in 1825). When the bones and teeth were found in England, people thought they had discovered a giant lizard at least 30 m (100 ft) long.

BUMP-NOSED RELATIVE

Muttaburrasaurus is one of the few dinosaurs discovered in Australia so far. It was a relative of *Iguanodon*, but slightly smaller at 7 m (23 ft) long. It had a strange, bony bump on its nose – no one yet knows what this was for.

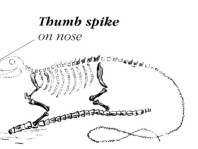

Thumb spike
on nose

One of the first drawings of *Iguanodon*

EARLY IDEAS

The first attempts to piece together an *Iguanodon* were quite wrong. They made it look like a giant lizard, with one spike placed on its nose like a horn. Then, in 1878, more than 30 complete *Iguanodon* fossils were found in a coal mine in Belgium. Experts were then able to learn much more about these dinosaurs.

SPIKED HANDS

Iguanodon had unusual hands. The three middle fingers had claws and looked like a hoof. The fifth finger could be bent, perhaps to hold food. *Iguanodon* had a sharp spike instead of a thumb. This could have helped the animal to defend itself.

Fifth finger bent across palm to grasp food

Group of *Iguanodon* feeding

Long, large head

FIND OUT MORE
THE HUMAN BODY: Hands
THE KINGDOM OF MAMMALS: Hooves

Horned Dinosaurs

An angry horned dinosaur such as *Triceratops* must have been a terrifying sight. These huge plant-eaters lived during the Cretaceous. They had massive heads, with large horns and bony neck frills. Horned dinosaurs were bulky with thick legs – some were as big as a rhinoceros. Few hunting dinosaurs would have dared to attack these armoured giants when they were fully grown.

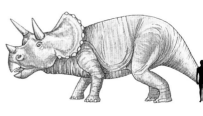

Triceratops: length 9 m (30 ft)

Tyrannosaurus

PROTECTING THE YOUNG

Triceratops was the largest horned dinosaur and weighed up to 10 tons. It probably lived in herds. If a fierce hunter such as *Tyrannosaurus* came near, a herd may have formed a circle around their young to protect them.

Neck frill formed from solid sheet of bone, with bony knobs around edge

Triceratops

Sharp, toothless beak for chopping off mouthfuls of leaves

DIFFERENT HEADS

Each type of horned dinosaur had a different arrangement of horns, and either short or long neck frills. *Styracosaurus* and *Centrosaurus* had short frills, but *Styracosaurus* had long spikes around the edge of its frill. The longer neck frill of *Chasmosaurus* was studded with spikes and knobs.

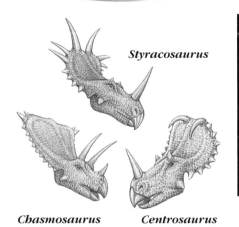

Styracosaurus

Chasmosaurus

Centrosaurus

AMAZING FACTS

★ *Torosaurus* had the largest skull of any known land animal – about 2.6 m (8½ ft) long, including an enormous frill.

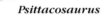

Tiny horn on cheek

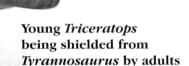

Young *Triceratops* being shielded from *Tyrannosaurus* by adults

Psittacosaurus

PARROT DINOSAUR

Psittacosaurus, a dinosaur found in Asia, was much lighter than other horned dinosaurs. It had no frill, and only a tiny horn on each cheek. However, its head was large, with a strong beak like a parrot's.

Forehead horn
1 m (3 ft) long

FIND OUT MORE
BIRDS: Parrots
THE KINGDOM OF MAMMALS:
Rhinoceros

Duckbill Dinosaurs

Parasaurolophus:
length 10 m (33 ft)

 Huge herds of duckbill dinosaurs (also called hadrosaurs) lived in many parts of the world in the late Cretaceous. They were enormous animals, up to 15 m (50 ft) long, and were the most common plant-eaters of the time. They had special beaks, similar to a duck's, and many had strange crests on their heads as well. The crests may have helped duckbills to recognise each other and may have made their calls louder.

LOUDER CALLS

Parasaurolophus had a long, hollow crest like a tube. Experts think that the crest made the dinosaur's calls louder and helped the sound go farther. This is how trumpets and other brass instruments work.

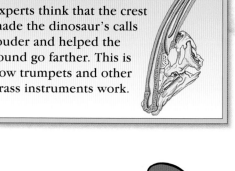

AMAZING FACTS

★ The duckbill dinosaur *Edmontosaurus* may have had as many as 1,000 teeth crowded into its mouth all at the same time.

CRESTED HEADS

Different kinds of duckbill had different shaped crests. Some were like fans, others more like horns. They may have produced different booming sounds, each kind of duckbill having its own call. Male and female crests may also have varied in size, shape and colour.

Saurolophus   *Lambeosaurus*   *Corythosaurus*

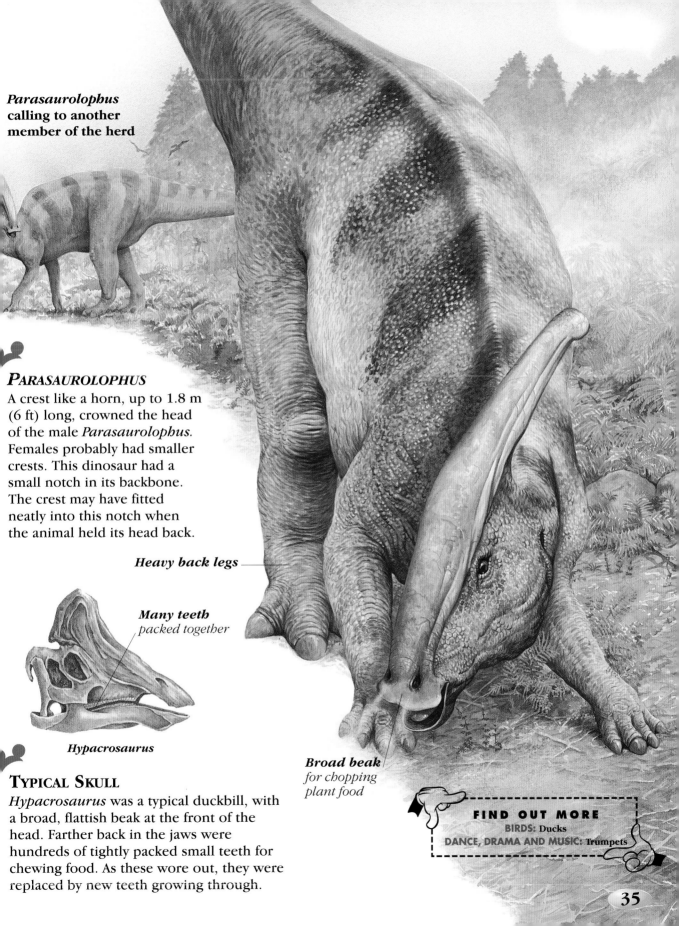

**Parasaurolophus
calling to another
member of the herd**

PARASAUROLOPHUS

A crest like a horn, up to 1.8 m
(6 ft) long, crowned the head
of the male *Parasaurolophus.*
Females probably had smaller
crests. This dinosaur had a
small notch in its backbone.
The crest may have fitted
neatly into this notch when
the animal held its head back.

Heavy back legs —

Many teeth
packed together

Hypacrosaurus

TYPICAL SKULL

Hypacrosaurus was a typical duckbill, with
a broad, flattish beak at the front of the
head. Farther back in the jaws were
hundreds of tightly packed small teeth for
chewing food. As these wore out, they were
replaced by new teeth growing through.

Broad beak
*for chopping
plant food*

FIND OUT MORE
BIRDS: Ducks
DANCE, DRAMA AND MUSIC: Trumpets

The Family Life of Dinosaurs

Like most reptiles, dinosaurs laid eggs, but fossil nests of only a few kinds of dinosaur have been found. Most of what we know about dinosaur family life comes from the duckbill dinosaur nests discovered in the U.S..

These amazing finds show that the duckbill *Maiasaura* made large, round nests of earth. Each mound had a dip in the center where up to 20 eggs were laid. The eggs were then covered with earth and leaves to keep them warm. Some birds and crocodiles today bury their eggs in this way. Each *Maiasaura* egg probably weighed about 1 kg (2 lb). A newly hatched baby *Maiasaura* was only about 35 cm (14 in) long.

DINOSAUR EGGS

Like other reptiles, dinosaurs laid their eggs on land. Such eggs needed hard or leathery shells to keep the babies safe until they hatched. Some dinosaur eggs were round. Others were oval, or long and thin.

Baby dinosaur inside egg

Nest mound
containing eggs

SAFETY IN NUMBERS

An 80-million-year-old *Maiasaura* nest site was found in Montana in 1978. It contained about 40 nests, showing that the dinosaur nested in groups. While some members of the herd were feeding, others could watch the eggs and young. The dinosaurs may even have brought food to their young.

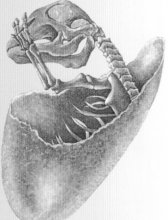

Fossilized baby *Maiasaura* in its egg

Newly hatched
baby Maiasaura

Adult Maiasaura
guarding nest

NEATLY SPACED NESTS

The *Maiasaura* nests found in
Montana were spaced about
7 m (23 ft) apart. This left room
for each mother to get to her
nest, or to lie alongside it. Each
nest was about 2 m (6 ft) wide.

Group of *Maiasaura*
looking after nests
and young

Female Maiasaura
feeding her young

FIND OUT MORE
BIRDS: Nest building
REPTILES AND AMPHIBIANS: Crocodiles

Bonehead Dinosaurs

Although they were peaceful plant-eaters most of the time, rival male bonehead dinosaurs probably took part in fierce headbutting battles in the breeding season. Just like bighorn sheep today, they probably fought to win females, by banging their thickened skulls together. These dinosaurs lived in the Cretaceous. They were up to 5 m (16 ft) long and moved on two back legs.

Stegoceras:
length 2 m (7 ft)

AMAZING FACTS

★ The dome on the head of *Pachycephalosaurus*, the largest bonehead, could be 25 cm (10 in) thick. Its dome got bigger as the animal aged.

BONY HEADS

Some boneheads, such as *Prenocephale* and *Stygimoloch*, had a dome of solid bone on top of the skull. Others, like *Homalocephale*, had flatter heads, although the bone was still very thick. Most boneheads also had lots of knobs and spikes on the head.

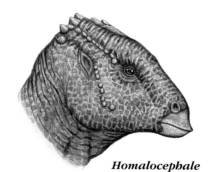

Homalocephale

Female sheltering her young

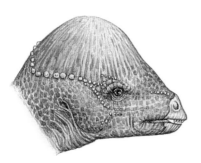

Prenocephale

Stygimoloch

DOMED SKULL

The skull of *Pachycephalosaurus* was about 50 cm (20 in) long. It had bony knobs at the back and spikes on the nose. The jaws of this dinosaur were filled with jagged-edged teeth for shredding plants.

Bony knobs

Spikes *on nose*

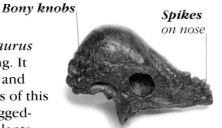

Pachycephalosaurus **skull**

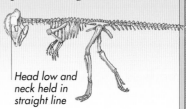

STRONG SKELETON

This *Stegoceras* skeleton is in the headbutting position. Special joints strengthened the bones of the back and stopped them from twisting out of place during battles.

Head low and neck held in straight line

Backbone *strengthened by bony rods*

Dome of *solid bone*

Tail held *out straight*

Head lowered, *ready for collision*

Powerful legs

BATTLING DINOSAURS

Rival male *Stegoceras* dinosaurs charged each other with their heads lowered and their tails held straight out behind. As they met head-on, their bony skulls took most of the force of the clash, so the dinosaurs did not suffer too much damage.

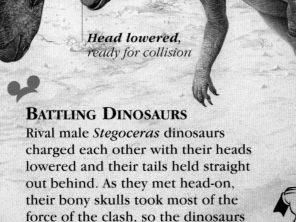

FIND OUT MORE
THE HUMAN BODY: Bones, Skulls

Battling *Stegoceras* dinosaurs

Armoured Dinosaurs

Ankylosaurus:
length 8 m (26 ft)

☞ **A**rmoured dinosaurs had their own built-in defenses, like tanks. They were studded with spikes and slabs of bone. Some also had a bony club on the end of the tail to fight off their enemies. These plant-eaters lived from mid-Jurassic times through to the late Cretaceous. They were up to 8 m (26 ft) long and had barrel-shaped bodies and short, sturdy legs.

A DANGEROUS WEAPON

The tail of *Ankylosaurus* was more than 2 m (7 ft) long and tipped with a heavy club made of two balls of bone joined together. This dinosaur could lash its tail from side to side, hitting an enemy with its club.

SPIKY DEFENSES

There were two types of armoured dinosaur. Rows of fearsome spikes on their sides made nodosaurs, such as *Edmontonia*, hard to attack. The ankylosaurs, such as *Saichania*, also had bony clubs on their tails.

Back covered
with protective
spikes and
bony plates

Bony club

Saichania

Edmontonia

BONY PLATES

The leathery skin of an ankylosaur was armoured with bony plates. Large plates protected the neck and shoulders, while smaller plates lined the tail. Only the underside of the dinosaur was not armoured.

Fossil of bony plate

EYE PROTECTORS

Even the eyes of an ankylosaur had shutters of bone that came down over the normal eyelids, protecting the eyes underneath.

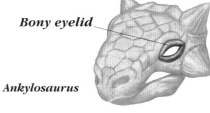

Bony eyelid

Tyrannosaurus

Ankylosaurus

AMAZING FACTS

★ With its heavy armour, a typical ankylosaur weighed at least 2 tons. The bony tail club alone weighed as much as 30 kg (65 lb) – the same as the average 10-year-old child.

A blow from the bony club could break the leg of a Tyrannosaurus

Sharp spikes guarded the sides of Ankylosaurus

Ankylosaurus protecting itself with its tail

Strong, sturdy legs to support the heavy body

FIND OUT MORE
THE HUMAN BODY: Bones, Skin

Plated Dinosaurs

Plated dinosaurs, or stegosaurs, were heavy, lumbering creatures with rows of bony plates on the back and tail. The plates may have helped them control their body temperature. These plant-eaters lived in the Jurassic and Cretaceous. They usually walked on four legs, but most could probably rear up on their back legs to feed on leaves in trees.

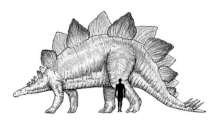

Stegosaurus:
length 9 m (30 ft)

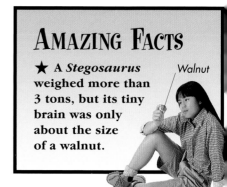

AMAZING FACTS

★ A *Stegosaurus* weighed more than 3 tons, but its tiny brain was only about the size of a walnut.

Walnut

Kentrosaurus

Tail spikes for swinging at attacker

Tuojiangosauru[s]

WHERE WERE THE PLATES?

No one knows how the plates were arranged on *Stegosaurus*, because they were embedded in the skin, and not attached to the skeleton. When fossils are found, often the plates are scattered all over the place, or even missing.

Some experts once thought the plates lay flat in pairs, like armour

Most experts now think the plates stood upright, to catch the sun or the breeze

BROAD AND NARROW PLATES

Each type of stegosaur had different shaped plates. *Stegosaurus* had broad plates. *Kentrosaurus* and *Tuojiangosaurus* had much narrower plates, like large spikes. They both also had spikes on their shoulders and tails, which would have helped protect them.

STOMACH STONES

Experts think big plant-eating dinosaurs such as stegosaurs swallowed stones to grind food up in their stomachs.

Stomach stones found with fossil of big plant-eater

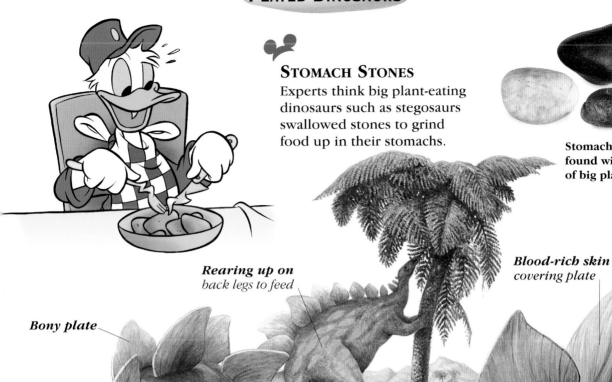

Blood-rich skin covering plate

Rearing up on back legs to feed

Bony plate

TEMPERATURE CONTROL

The plates on a *Stegosaurus* were covered in blood-rich skin. If the dinosaur turned so the plates faced the sun, the blood would be warmed. If the dinosaur turned so the plates were in a cool breeze, the blood would lose heat.

Group of *Stegosaurus*

FIND OUT MORE
THE HUMAN BODY: Blood
REPTILES AND AMPHIBIANS: Body heat

Dinosaur Discoveries

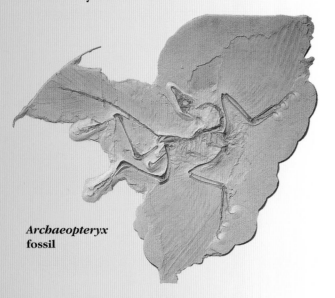

Until the 19th century, no one knew what dinosaur bones were. Then experts realised they must once have belonged to giant reptiles that no longer lived on Earth.

Since then, dinosaur remains have been found on every continent, and there are certainly many yet to be discovered. New techniques allow experts to find out more than ever before from the fossil bones, footprints and even dinosaur dung. Non-dinosaur fossils are important, too. The first identified fossil of *Archaeopteryx*, the first known bird, was discovered in Germany in 1861.

Archaeopteryx fossil

FOSSIL HUNTING

Most early dinosaur discoveries were made in Europe and North America. In the first part of the 20th century, there were important finds in China and Mongolia. Today, experts are discovering dinosaur bones in areas such as Africa and Antarctica, which were little explored in the past.

North America
More dinosaurs have been discovered in the U.S. than in any other country, and new ones are still being found. Large numbers of Late Cretaceous dinosaur fossils have also been found in Canada, particularly in Alberta.

North America

South America
About 50 different dinosaurs have been discovered in South America, mostly in Argentina. The most famous South American expert is the Argentinian José Bonaparte, who named the carnosaur Carnotaurus.

South America

Riojasaurus

Map showing where dinosaur fossils have been found

Edward Cope

RIVAL BONE HUNTERS

Wealthy 19th-century North American dinosaur fossil collectors Edward Drinker Cope and Othniel Marsh were bitter rivals. Each tried to find more new dinosaurs than the other – in total they named nearly 130 different dinosaurs.

Asia

A great many dinosaurs have been discovered in Asia, particularly in Mongolia and China. More than 100 kinds of dinosaurs have been found in China, many by Chinese experts such as Dong Zhiming.

Europe

Dinosaur fossils have been found all over Europe, especially in France, Britain and Germany. Dinosaur remains were first identified as such in Britain, in the 1820s.

Europe

Megalosaurus

Asia

Barapasaurus

Africa

Heterodontosaurus

Australia and Antarctica

Only a few dinosaurs have so far been found in Australia, mostly in Queensland. Antarctica is only now being explored, but fossils of armoured and other dinosaurs are being found there.

Australia

Minmi

Africa

Some of the most exciting recent dinosaur finds have been in Africa. They include Carcharodontosaurus, the giant carnosaur found in northern Africa in 1995.

FIND OUT MORE

THE HUMAN BODY: Bones
PLANET EARTH: Fossils

Antarctica

Other Reptiles

The first reptiles appeared about 300 million years ago, a long time before the first dinosaurs. There were many kinds, from tiny creatures like lizards to heavy plant-eaters called rhynchosaurs. The rhynchosaurs died out at the end of the Triassic, when dinosaurs began their rule.

Hyperodapedon:
length 1.2 m (4 ft)

AMAZING FACTS

★ The 10 neck bones of *Tanystropheus* are so long that experts first thought they were the animal's leg bones.

FLYING LIZARD

Long-legged *Kuehneosaurus* could glide through the air. It did so with the help of two flaps of skin at the sides of its body. These flaps were supported by some extra-long ribs. *Kuehneosaurus* was about 65 cm (26 in) long from its nose to its tail.

STRONG-JAWED REPTILE

Heavy-bodied rhynchosaurs such as *Hyperodapedon* were common plant-eating reptiles during the Triassic. They had strong jaws and fed mostly on tough plants called seed ferns. When seed ferns died out in the late Triassic, rhynchosaurs disappeared, too.

Skin flaps held
out on long ribs

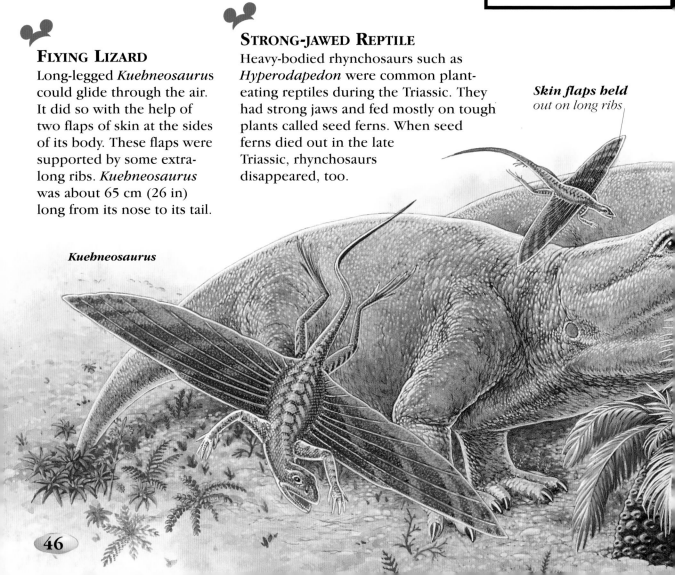

Kuehneosaurus

LONG-NECKED REPTILE

The Triassic reptile *Tanystropheus* was about 3 m (10 ft) long. Amazingly, its neck was longer than the whole body and tail added together. The long neck may have helped it to catch fish.

Long neck for reaching *out over the water to fish*

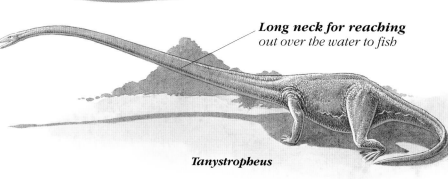

Tanystropheus

Hyperodapedon

Powerful jaw *for cropping plants*

Bony knobs along *back for protection*

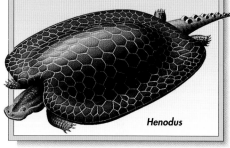

HARD-BEAKED REPTILE

Henodus was a sea reptile like a turtle, with a large bony shell. It probably fed on shellfish, which it crushed with its hard beak.

Henodus

Placodus

SHELLFISH-EATER

Placodus lived both on land and in the sea. It probably pulled shellfish off rocks with the teeth at the front of its jaws, then crushed them with the broad, flat teeth at the back.

FIND OUT MORE
WONDERS OF THE SEA: Shellfish
THE HUMAN BODY: Ribs

Flying Reptiles

Flying reptiles, or pterosaurs, took to the air 70 million years before any feathered birds appeared. They were the first animals able to fly, apart from insects. Unlike birds, flying reptiles had wings made of skin. They ranged from tiny, sparrow-sized creatures to giants the size of a small plane. Most had long, sharp jaws and caught fish, insects and other small animals.

Anhanguera:
wingspan 4 m (13 ft)

Long arm and
finger bones
supporting wing

FLYING FISH-EATER
Anhanguera lived in South America during the Cretaceous. Like all the pterosaurs, it had hollow bones, which were extremely light. It fed mostly on fish, which it could have scooped out of the water with its long, sharp-toothed jaws.

Wings
made
of skin

Anhanguera
may have used
wing-claws to
help it crawl

Anhanguera

MOVING ON LAND
Most experts think flying reptiles crawled using their wing-claws as well as their feet, but some think they walked upright like birds.

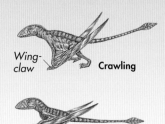

Wing-claw   Crawling

Walking upright

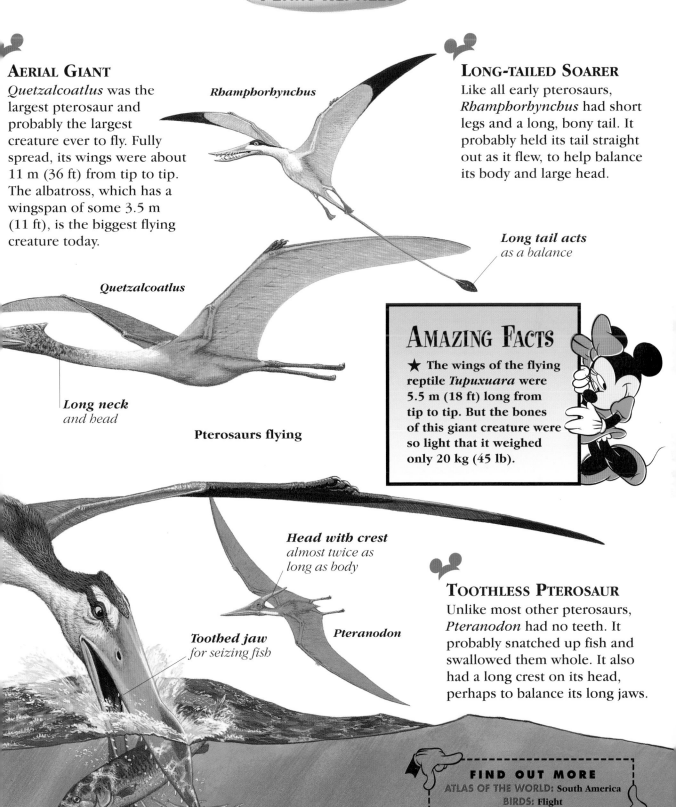

AERIAL GIANT

Quetzalcoatlus was the largest pterosaur and probably the largest creature ever to fly. Fully spread, its wings were about 11 m (36 ft) from tip to tip. The albatross, which has a wingspan of some 3.5 m (11 ft), is the biggest flying creature today.

Rhamphorhynchus

LONG-TAILED SOARER

Like all early pterosaurs, *Rhamphorhynchus* had short legs and a long, bony tail. It probably held its tail straight out as it flew, to help balance its body and large head.

Long tail acts *as a balance*

Quetzalcoatlus

Long neck *and head*

Pterosaurs flying

AMAZING FACTS

★ The wings of the flying reptile *Tupuxuara* were 5.5 m (18 ft) long from tip to tip. But the bones of this giant creature were so light that it weighed only 20 kg (45 lb).

Head with crest *almost twice as long as body*

Pteranodon

Toothed jaw *for seizing fish*

TOOTHLESS PTEROSAUR

Unlike most other pterosaurs, *Pteranodon* had no teeth. It probably snatched up fish and swallowed them whole. It also had a long crest on its head, perhaps to balance its long jaws.

FIND OUT MORE
ATLAS OF THE WORLD: South America
BIRDS: Flight

Sea Reptiles

While dinosaurs ruled the land, some reptiles began to live in the sea. Ichthyosaurs, plesiosaurs and pliosaurs were all large sea reptiles, with flippers instead of legs. Although they looked like fish, they had to come to the surface from time to time to breathe in air.

Shonisaurus:
length 15 m (50 ft)

HIGH-SPEED SWIMMER
Shonisaurus was the largest known ichthyosaur. It looked like a dolphin and ate fish and other sea creatures. Unlike most reptiles, *Shonisaurus* gave birth in the water to live young.

Belemnites, creatures like squid, were food for Shonisaurus

Skull up to
2.4 m (8 ft) long

Kronosaurus

FIERCE HUNTERS

With their huge, sharp-toothed jaws, pliosaurs were fierce hunters of large prey, even sharks. The biggest pliosaur was *Kronosaurus*.

AMAZING FACTS

★ This extraordinary fossil shows a female ichthyosaur giving birth. The baby is coming out tail first, like baby dolphins do today.

Fossil of baby ichthyosaur

Powerful tail

Neck longer
than body

FLYING UNDERWATER

Long-necked *Elasmosaurus* had four paddle-shaped flippers, which it flapped up and down like underwater wings. This plesiosaur spent most of its life at sea catching fish, but females came out onto land to lay eggs in pits on sandy beaches. *Elasmosaurus* was about 14 m (46 ft) long.

Streamlined body

Elasmosaurus

Paddle-shaped
flipper

ANCIENT SEA TURTLE

Archelon had huge flippers and a light shell, possibly covered with thick, rubbery skin. Up to 3.7 m (12 ft) long, it lived in the late Cretaceous.

Archelon

Shonisaurus

Long, slender snout
with small, sharp teeth

FIND OUT MORE
REPTILES AND AMPHIBIANS: Sea turtles
THE KINGDOM OF MAMMALS: Dolphins

Mammal-like Reptiles

☞ Before dinosaurs, reptiles that looked like mammals were common all over the world. The earliest of these mammal-like reptiles were pelycosaurs, some of which had huge sail-shaped fins on their backs. Later there were strong-jawed dicynodonts and cynodonts. Mammal-like reptiles began to die out in the late Triassic as dinosaurs and mammals became more common.

Cynognathus:
length 1 m (3 ft)

BEAKY PLANT-EATER

With its huge head and heavy body, *Kannemeyeria* looked fierce, but it was actually a plant-eater. Like other dicynodonts, it had only two teeth, but used its hard beak to tear up mouthfuls of tough roots and plants.

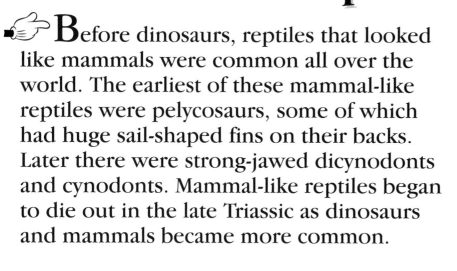

Kannemeyeria

DOGLIKE REPTILE

One of the largest cynodonts, *Cynognathus,* lived early in the Triassic. Its head looked like a dog's and it was a ferocious hunter. It may have fed on smaller reptiles.

Strong jaws
with a sharp set of teeth inside

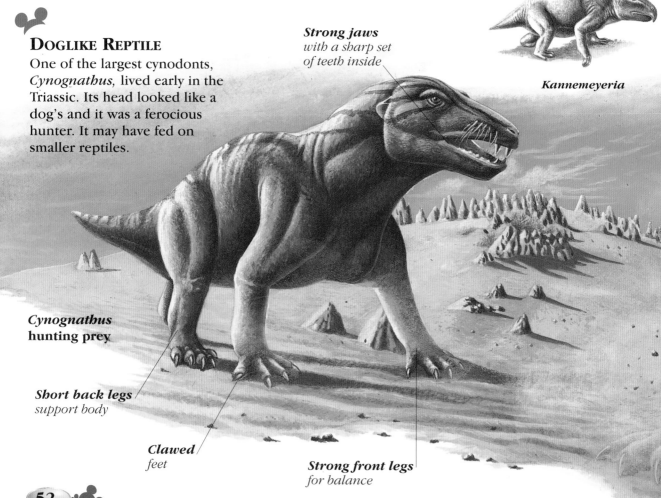

Cynognathus
hunting prey

Short back legs
support body

Clawed
feet

Strong front legs
for balance

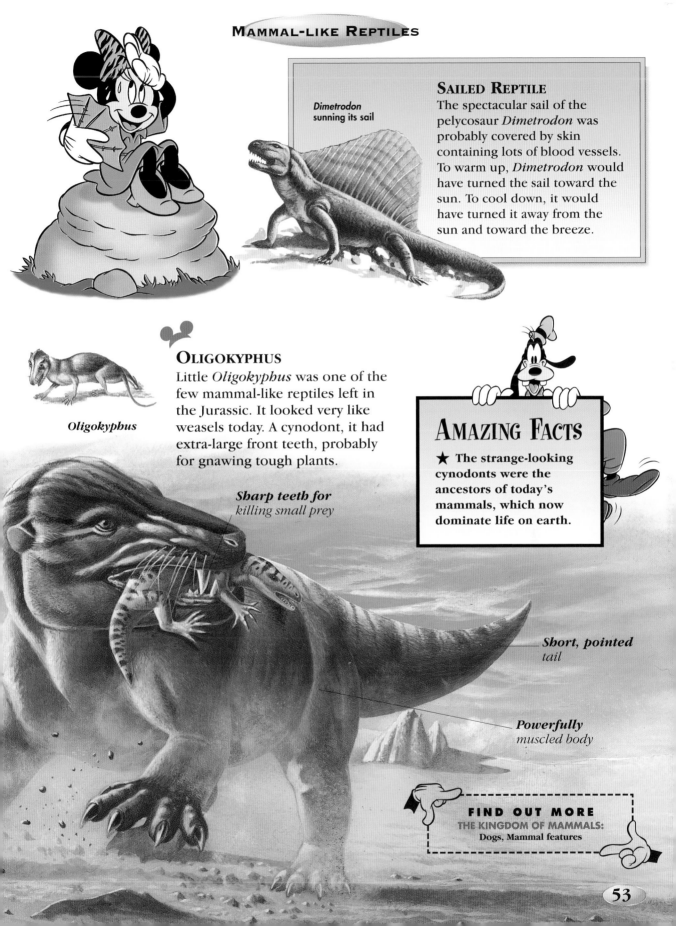

SAILED REPTILE

The spectacular sail of the pelycosaur *Dimetrodon* was probably covered by skin containing lots of blood vessels. To warm up, *Dimetrodon* would have turned the sail toward the sun. To cool down, it would have turned it away from the sun and toward the breeze.

Dimetrodon sunning its sail

OLIGOKYPHUS

Little *Oligokyphus* was one of the few mammal-like reptiles left in the Jurassic. It looked very like weasels today. A cynodont, it had extra-large front teeth, probably for gnawing tough plants.

Oligokyphus

Sharp teeth for *killing small prey*

AMAZING FACTS

★ The strange-looking cynodonts were the ancestors of today's mammals, which now dominate life on earth.

Short, pointed *tail*

Powerfully *muscled body*

FIND OUT MORE
THE KINGDOM OF MAMMALS:
Dogs, Mammal features

The End of the Dinosaurs

Did a huge meteorite strike Earth 65 million years ago and kill off the dinosaurs by darkening the world's skies? Most experts believe this is what happened.

The main evidence for the meteorite idea is a huge crater found in Mexico. Many other theories about what killed the dinosaurs have been proposed, but a giant meteorite is the most likely one. It may be, though, that the dinosaurs were already slowly dying out, because the world's climates were gradually becoming more extreme as the continents drifted farther apart.

A BOLT FROM SPACE

The remains of a huge crater about 200 km (125 miles) across was found in Mexico in 1990. It was probably made by a giant meteorite 65 million years ago. Such a meteorite could have been 10 km (6 miles) wide and thrown up enough dust and vapour to darken skies all over the world.

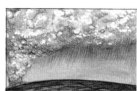

Dust and water vapour fill the sky, blocking out sunlight all over the world.

Plants and animals die from the intense cold and lack of sunlight.

Later, the dust settles and vapour clouds trap the sun's heat, killing more animals.

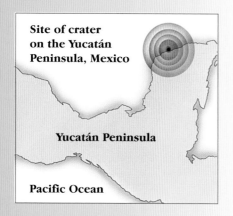

Site of crater on the Yucatán Peninsula, Mexico

Yucatán Peninsula

Pacific Ocean

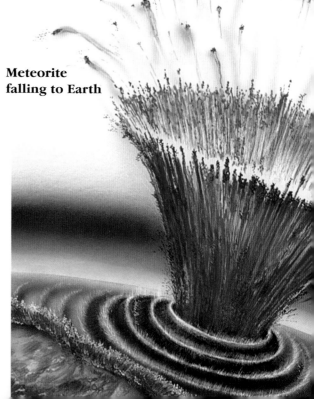

Meteorite falling to Earth

WHAT DISAPPEARED?

Not just dinosaurs disappeared at the end of the Cretaceous. Flying reptiles, sea reptiles and ammonites were also lost forever at this time.

WHAT SURVIVED?

Some reptiles, such as crocodiles, managed to live through whatever happened 65 million years ago. Birds, mammals, most insects, and amphibians also survived.

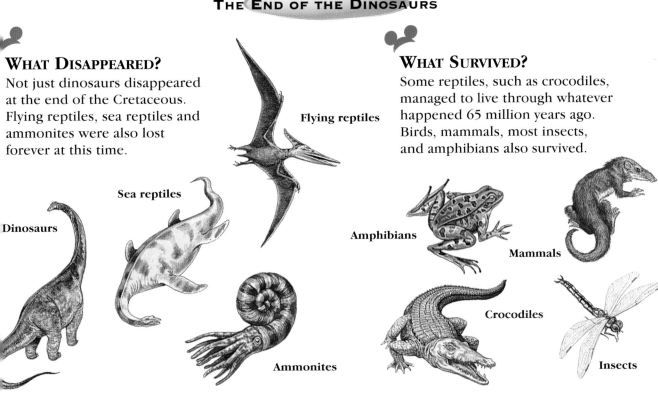

Flying reptiles

Sea reptiles

Dinosaurs

Ammonites

Amphibians

Mammals

Crocodiles

Insects

Flaming path of the falling meteorite

Dust and vapour thrown up by the meteorite's impact

VOLCANIC ACTIVITY

Some experts believe that huge volcanic eruptions killed off the dinosaurs. The eruptions would have filled the skies with thick clouds of dust in much the same way that a huge meteorite might have done.

Ash billowing from an erupting volcano, Hawaii

FIND OUT MORE
PLANET EARTH: Volcanoes
SPACE: Meteoroids

Glossary of Key Words

Ammonite: A sea-living animal with a spiral shell that became extinct about 65 million years ago. Ammonite shells exist today, but only as fossils.

Armoured dinosaur: A type of dinosaur covered with bony plates, spikes and knobs to protect it from danger. There were two types of armoured dinosaur – ankylosaurs and nodosaurs.

Boneheaded dinosaur: A type of plant-eating dinosaur with a thick dome of bone on its skull.

Cannibal: An animal that eats its own kind.

Carnosaur: A type of large, meat-eating dinosaur.

Ceratosaur: A type of small, meat-eating dinosaur.

Climate: The normal weather patterns of a particular region.

Coelurosaur: A type of slender, fast-moving, meat-eating dinosaur.

Continent: One of the seven main areas of land on Earth.

Cretaceous period: The time from 135 to 65 million years ago in the Mesozoic era. Dinosaurs were the most varied in this period, but became extinct by the end of it.

Cycad: A cone-bearing, palm-like plant that lived before flowering plants. It was most common during the Mesozoic era.

Cynodont: A type of mammal-like reptile with strong jaws and powerful muscles; the ancestor of today's mammals.

Dromaeosaur: A type of fast-running, meat-eating dinosaur, with large curved claws on each back foot.

Duckbilled dinosaur: A type of large, plant-eating dinosaur with a long, flat beak; also called a hadrosaur.

Fern: A green plant, usually with long, feathery leaves, or fronds. Some ferns have short stems and grow close to the ground, but others can grow as tall as trees.

Fossil: The remains of a plant or animal preserved in rock. Impressions in rock, such as footprints or skin, can also become fossilized.

Hadrosaur: Another name for duckbilled dinosaur.

Horned dinosaur: A type of dinosaur with a large head, long pointed horns and a bony frill at the back of its skull.

Ichthyosaur: A type of fast-swimming, sea-living reptile that looked like the dolphins of today.

Iguanodon: A type of large, plant-eating dinosaur with a sharp thumb spike on each hand.

Jurassic period: The time from 205 to 135 million years ago in the Mesozoic era.

Mammal: A warm-blooded animal with a backbone, which gives birth to live babies and feeds them on milk.

Mesozoic era: The time from 250 to 65 million years ago. Third of the four eras that have taken place since the Earth was formed, it is made up of three periods – the Triassic, Jurassic and Cretaceous.

Meteorite: A piece of rock that has travelled through Space and fallen to Earth, often forming a crater where it lands.

Ornithomimid: A type of fast-running, meat-eating dinosaur that looked like the ostriches of today.

Paleontologist: A scientist who studies fossils and extinct creatures, such as dinosaurs.

Pangaea: The name given to the one huge continent that existed during the Triassic period.

Pelycosaur: A type of mammal-like reptile. Pelycosaurs had huge sail-shaped fins on their backs.

Plated dinosaur: A type of heavy, plant-eating dinosaur with rows of bony plates along its back and tail.

Plesiosaur: A type of sea-living reptile with a long neck and flipper-like limbs. It laid its eggs on land.

Pliosaur: A type of sea-living reptile with a large head and jaw. Pliosaurs caught large prey, such as sharks.

Pterosaur: A type of flying reptile that lived at the same time as the dinosaurs, with wings of skin attached to extra-long arm and finger bones.

Reptile: A cold-blooded animal with four legs, a backbone and scaly skin. Reptiles lay eggs.

Rhynchosaur: A type of heavy-bodied, plant-eating reptile that lived during the Triassic period.

Sauropod: A type of long-necked, plant-eating dinosaur. Sauropods were the largest dinosaurs.

Stegosaur: A type of plated dinosaur with a double row of bony plates along its back.

Triassic period: The time from 250 to 205 million years ago in the Mesozoic era. Dinosaurs first appeared on Earth at the end of this period.

Index

Acknowledgments

AUTHOR
Jinny Johnson

CONSULTANTS FOR DINOSAURS
Michael J. Benton is Professor of Vertebrate Palaeontology in
the Department of Geology at the University of Bristol, England.
He has lectured at the Queen's University of Belfast and
was Junior Research Fellow at Trinity College, Oxford,
and has written and consulted on numerous books about
dinosaurs for both children and adults.
Barry Cox is Professor of Zoology at King's College in London,
England. He has been involved in expeditions to research
fossils and their distribution in Central Africa, Argentina,
Brazil and Australia.

EDUCATIONAL CONSULTANTS
Lois Eskin, BSc, is a publishing consultant with special expertise
in organizational planning, research and product planning for
educational publishers.
Kurt W. Fischer, PhD, Professor at Harvard University,
Graduate School of Education.

INTERNATIONAL CONSULTANTS
Pamela Katherina Decho, BA (Hons), is a consultant editor
specializing in Latin America.
Zahara Wan is a consultant editor specializing in Southeast Asia.
Minghua Zhao, PhD, MSc, MA, BA, is a consultant editor
specializing in China and East Asia.

ILLUSTRATORS
Daniel Biddulph, Bill Donohoe, James Field,
Roy Flooks, Liz Gray, Nick Hall, Steve Kirk,
Martin Knowelden, Kevin Maddison, Andrew Robinson,
Peter D. Scott, Guy Smith, Dan Wright.
Disney art colouring: Neil Rigby.

FOR DISNEY ARTWORK IN THIS BOOK
Franco Valussi
With special thanks to Michael Horowitz
and Carson Van Osten

AGENCY PHOTOGRAPHS
21 Francois Gohier/Ardea, London; 45 Courtesy of
the Peabody Museum of Natural History, Yale University;
51 Pat Morris/Ardea, London; 55 ZEFA/Stockmarket;
18, 19, 22, 26, 29, 31, 39, 41, 43, & 44 are all from
the Natural History Museum, London.

CHILDREN'S PHOTOGRAPHS
Ray Moller

PROJECT MANAGEMENT FOR DISNEY
With special thanks to Cally Chambers

PROJECT MANAGEMENT FOR PAPERVIEW
Isabelle Demolin, Delphine Prinselaar

COVER DESIGN
Louise Laurent